*Place right hand here
and close cover*

By the Same Author

Crosswords For The Bath
Spa Trivia
The Book of OB
Bogor, Vols. 1-12

In Preparation

The Extremely Naughty Victorian Hand Book
Erotic Pleasures Of The Foot

THE NAUGHTY VICTORIAN

OMNIA SUNT AMABILIA INSANA

HAND BOOK

THE REDISCOVERED ART OF EROTIC HAND MANIPULATION

Hidden 'mongst your folds and creases
Lurk Sir Passion's wicked nieces.

Henry Quill-Smith

First published in Great Britain 1989
Text copyright © 1989 by Burton Silver
Illustrations copyright © 1989 by Jeremy Bennett

Bloomsbury Publishing Limited
2 Soho Square, London W1V 5DE

ISBN 0-7475-0420-2

Grateful thanks to the trustees for
access to the Sladden Lynch collection.

Devised and originated by Silverculture Press,
487 Karaka Bay Rd. Wellington 3, New Zealand.

Book design and production by
Trevor Plaisted, Wellington.

Printed in Hong Kong through
Bookprint Consultants Ltd, Wellington.

THE NAUGHTY VICTORIAN

HAND BOOK

THE REDISCOVERED ART OF EROTIC HAND MANIPULATION

BY BURTON SILVER
ILLUSTRATED BY JEREMY BENNETT

BLOOMSBURY

Dr Cornelius Ogle and family. December 1889.

FOREWORD

BY DR CORNELIUS OGLE

From an address given to
The West London Scientific Association,
October, 1889

AS A DOCTOR I cannot speak too highly of this book of original engravings, which, by the simple contrivance of holes auspiciously placed, affords an entertainment most enjoyable and vitalising. However, let me at once warrant that the purpose of this work is not merely to amuse and entertain, but, in so doing, to assuage the sorrow of the heart, lift the load of melancholy from the desponding mind, and restore to the wounded spirit its wonted elasticity. Indeed it has been my pleasure to demonstrate the workings of this fine book to more than a few patients, and I can assure you that even when a severe prudery was evident, *I have never experienced a failure*. The appropriate fervours have always been quickly aroused and harmlessly released in a manner most therapeutic and becoming.

I have heard it urged that by exposing manifestations of carnality in the reader's own hand, this book will encourage illicit gratification of the passions and promote a corruption of the vital juices. Such prejudice I contend is most underserved and unwarrantable. In no way does this work constitute a source of moral contagion.

I entertain a firm and well-founded conviction that nothing is more productive of happiness and amusement than the flesh when exposed by accident. Conversely, when revealed with intent to excite, nothing is more fruitful of misery. A careful examination of the scenes contained in these pages will show garments to have been variously disarranged through inadvertence or innocent accident, thus encouraging a healthy mirth and merriment. Far from there being an increase of dangerous and degenerative tension consequent upon the excitement induced by these most real images of bared flesh, it is instead dissipated and relieved harmlessly through laughter.

Indeed after only one session with this book, many of my patients have experienced violent explosions of mirth and a consequent release of tension just when the risks of a licentious detumescence seemed inevitable. Truly it has been said that laughter's vibration is the law of life, and I think you will allow to yourselves that these engravings deliver a most joyful and exciting experience, the like of which is seldom if ever to be had today without the unfortunate accompaniment of lustful immodesties.

In conclusion, permit me to suggest the regular use of this book as a tonic: two or three exposures prior to retiring each night cannot fail but to purge the mind of unhealthy urges and restore to the body its vital powers.

Cornelius Ogle

INTRODUCTION

TO STUDY THE ART of erotic hand manipulation is to start out on a wonderful journey of discovery, a journey that leads into a world of secret folds and furrows. An exciting world, so immense and varied that it is impossible to explore all its voluptuous manifestations. A world that, once discovered, can never be forgotten. But this is not a journey we need make alone. To help us unravel the intricacies of the art, we are expertly guided by beautiful engravings, rendered in such a way that only we can make them meaningful and give them life.

Perhaps it was the interactive nature of this art that the narrow morality of Victorian England found so threatening; this "promotion of erotic complicity with the artist" that led to its withdrawal from sale and relegation to the Private Case Catalogue. For no matter whether this work was billed as a "medicinal contrivance for the diminished urge" or simply as a harmless parlourgame, the prudish Victorian mind would have intuitively grasped the contagious nature of its underlying message. To hide behind shock and indignation would no longer have been possible, for the art of erotic hand manipulation tricked them into "active licentious collaboration". Worse still, by encouraging them to recognise the voluptuous potential of their own, up until now, quite innocent fingers, it became the wicked seducer, stealing away "the hand's precious virginity". Today such attitudes are laughable but, as you will find, these engravings have lost none of their power to excite and provoke.

This book deals with the more delicate, lighthearted aspects of erotic hand manipulation, revealing its magic in a straightforward way that will help toward a deeper understanding of our own and others' sensuality. This makes it ideal for the beginner who wishes to enter the powerful world of the exposed engraving and explore for the first time the furtler's inspired craft. To assist the novice further, useful notes are included on ways in which the positions may be enhanced and embellished, and not just for the eye alone. These engravings induce powerful statements of tactile value where the reader is encouraged to delight in the sensation of touch — as if the body were in miniature and the finger tip the caressing palm.

Above all, this book will allow readers of all ages and cultures to discover a unique and sensuous part of themselves. A part that is never more than an arm's length away and always more real than any video image.

INSTRUCTIONS
How to use the Hand Book

Fig I. Lay book on a firm surface. With the right hand, adopt the hand shape shown, as in fig I below for example.

Fig II. While maintaining this shape, lift **two** pages and position the right hand directly under the illustration of the hand.

Fig III. Turn the top page to expose. Make final adjustments with your hand as appropriate.

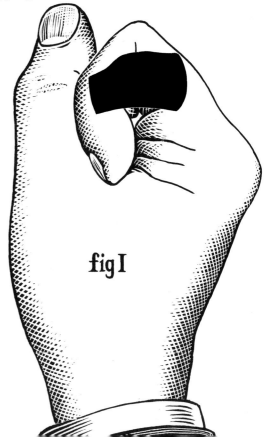

EROTIC HAND MANIPULATION

Origins & Etymology

THE ORIGINS of erotic hand manipulation, or "furtling" as it was known in Britain, are shrouded in mystery. It is probable that men and women throughout the ages have knowingly examined the erotic creases and folds in their own and others' hands, but just when this enjoyable pastime was combined with design to transform it into an art form is unclear. There is some evidence that furtling tablets — thin rectangles of hardwood bearing a simple carved design and an appropriately placed aperture — were used for public display as early as the fourteenth century. Certainly small boxed furtling sets were known in the sixteenth century, and even then were collectors' items.

But it was not until improvement in the quality of illustration reproduction, which followed the introduction of white line engraving on wood, that the art of erotic hand manipulation looked like becoming widely available in book form. Prior to the middle of the eighteenth century the economics of book production had meant the use of coarsely cut woodcuts that suited cheap paper. But the engraving, with its intricate pattern of white lines, could now perfectly echo the fingers' fine whorls and thus produce strikingly complementary effects of far greater appeal.

Unfortunately this was also a time of great sexual repression and initial attempts to publish books of "engravings for exposure", even in strictly limited editions, led to unprecedented moral outrage that resulted in many books being voluntarily withdrawn by wary publishers. At the same time photography was now able to meet the growing market for cheap high-quality erotic pictures, with studies of nudes in magazines like *The Exquisite* being available from as early as 1842. Later, when the moral climate was more permissive, and the art of erotic hand manipulation could well have fulfilled the need for realistic moving images of a sensuous nature, cinematography was sweeping all before it.

As is often the case, the nomenclature of the art has survived better than the art itself. Names for the various hand positions and their related erotic aspects were well established in Britain by the middle of the eighteenth century. However, it was not until 1844, with the brief appearance of Doctor McGill's *The Promiscuous Palm*, that a serious attempt was made to formalise and systematise them to provide an easy reference system. Two years later an excellent private collection of "scenes for exposure", said to belong to John Greenmore, owner of the Evans Super Club, was collated into a strictly limited edition called *The Erotic Language Of The Hand*. This now standard work contained not only the Latin terms but also the common names. It seems likely, however, that the furore engendered by the publication of *The Promiscuous Palm* and later *The Book Of Holes* in the United States would have seen some attempt to opt for less offensive names where possible.

Erotic hand manipulation was, after all, the preserve of the Victorian upper classes who struck a delicately aesthetic pose in matters of the flesh, and whose language showed a great restraint in contrast to social events which revealed the beginnings of a major moral revolution. Even the name "furtling", undoubtedly derived from "furtive", is suggestive of something to be practised in secret.

It may well be, therefore, that where the common name was regarded as too crude or obvious, it was simply rendered as a translation of the Latin, as in the case of The Crocodile, prudishly shortened from *Crocodilus libidinosus*.

There is good evidence to suggest that the Latin nomenclature may have predated and therefore influenced the names in common usage. *Botellus pudicus* is a good example. *Botellus* is a small pudding sausage and *pudicus* means chaste. Literally translated this aspect is intriguingly described as a small chaste pudding sausage, obviously referring to the sausage-like piece of compressed skin so formed. It seems an unlikely coincidence that the common name, Bot Pudding, shares the same first syllables of the Latin names in spite of having its own etymological validity — Bot being short for bottom, and Pudding a well-known euphemism for the lower front unmentionables.

While many of the terms describe the visual aspect of the manipulated hand, they also tend to have an erotic relevance. Thus Pinky Puff obviously relates to the flushed and puffed-up nature of the side of the finger when compressed. But a puff is also a tartlet, and the word "tart", a contraction of "sweetheart", was used in Victorian times to apply to a girl of loose morals. A name like Peepeye quite clearly refers to the "naughty peephole" made by the finger and thumb in this position, but may well also be rhyming slang for thigh, for which this aspect is often used.

Many names are still known, but many more, along with descriptions of their aspects, have sadly disappeared. However, now that the art of erotic hand manipulation has been rediscovered, it will undoubtedly enjoy a renaissance, and staid Victorian terms are likely to change in favour of richer euphemisms, more appropriate in this enlightened age.

This exposure may be most agreeably embellished by the tight squeezing of the index finger, thus engendering a pleasing crimson glow typical of the flesh when recently immersed in hot water.

CORRESPONDENCE

1889-1890
*Letters of commendation,
information and damnation*

I have now had your book for upward of two months and cannot say enough in its praise. Having long been afflicted by an embarrassing debility of my vital powers, I am indebted to you for providing such a portable companion, that I may open it, and straightway by the application of my hand to the holes so provided, achieve, upon viewing the result, a restoration of my powers of quite unexpected force.

Sir Archibald Drew

I am profoundly grateful that a subject of such importance should be treated in a manner at once so noble and so delicate. Any pure-minded teacher or mother may safely leave this book in the presence of young children without the slightest chance of their small hands being able to render the illustrations improper. There is thus no fear that their fragile sensibilities may be wounded or that they may be encouraged in the practice of luxuries.

Mrs Laura Pemberton

I have been gratified to see that those who in past times have viewed unsightly irregularities in their hands with dismay may take delight in the exciting possibilities your hand book now affords them. Sufferers of warts, eczema, scabies, and those with moles, nicotine stains or large haired areas, will of a sudden find themselves in great demand where the hand book is produced in company.

Dr Ernest Puddick

While my whole family has found your book in an eminent degree vitalising, it is nevertheless my duty to warn that distressing effects of an immodest nature may be obtained by its improper use. Recently my nephew placed the apertures over his mouth and was seen to observe the degrading results in a mirror. I should say he was profoundly thrashed for this perversion.

Mrs Constance Cringle

Might I be permitted to submit to your notice a most admirable embellishment suggested recently by an acquaintance of mine. Exciting crimson welts such as those occasioned by spanking may be readily obtained if the thumbnail is pressed firmly into the appropriate area for a few moments prior to applying the hand to the hole.

Colonel Oliver Pratt

I have not the slightest wish to suggest your book is anything but of the highest moral purpose, yet I must own that our gardener, a sober man of perfectly good manners, became unusually flushed and animated when he happened upon it in the conservatory last evening. He was later seen by the maid to attack his hand in a most persistently passionate manner, occasioning such brusing that I fear he will be unable to dig on the morrow. I beg your confirmation by return that this book is not wisely demonstrated to those of the servant class.

Lady Jane Aldershaw

While I have found this contrivance most efficacious in all respects, might I suggest the axilla as a suitable subject for future editions. I am sure my wife and I are not alone in deriving considerable therapy from this much neglected area.

C. Jimkins, Esq.

The hand was not meant for this, sir. A gross transmogrification to be thoroughly reviled. You and your depraved readers would do well to let the phrase "Corruptio optimi pessima" ring about your ears.

Rev. F. B. Cummings, M.A.

How gratifying it was to find my hands were no longer simply turners of the page. What delight they now took in diving between the sheets and becoming active participants in the effect; not just visually adding colour and tone, but providing also shape, texture and movement, such that I was rewarded with an endless variety of erotic surprise of a type most vitalising and becoming.

Miss Mildred Perkins

If any inducement were required to persuade us to the consideration of the degrading effects of this book, we need look no further than the unfortunate case of my aunt. A spinster of sixty-four years, and sound in body and mind, she is nevertheless of an emotional maturity not in keeping with her age. Her brother, my uncle, thoughtlessly introduced her to the ways of your vile book some four weeks ago, and so profound was the defiling effect upon her delicate spirit, she has since quite refused to remove her gloves, even whilst bathing.

Mrs H.T. Squillwater

I feel compelled to express my deepest concern at the widespread popularity your hand book seems to be enjoying. I firmly hold that furtling is rightly the preserve of those of the higher classes who are possessed of sufficient emotional and intellectual maturity to fortify them against any contamination by this most subtle of art forms. While I am gratified to see that some of the more advanced positions are not included in your collection, I am sure it is only a matter of time before aspects such as *Fundamentum activum* are discovered and spread amongst the masses, with the gravest of consequences. Indeed, I have it on good authority that single pages torn from your book are being sold most cheaply and quite openly in the poorer areas of London. Worse still, people are not only daubing their hands with all manner of paints in order to obtain lewd effects, but have been seen to insert objects of various kinds into their folds for the sake of so-called amusement. Not only is the art of erotic hand manipulation being thus desecrated, but these poor spirits are in constant danger of overexciting their passions and yielding to the deleterious effects of unchecked lust.

Sir Ernest Larchings, Bart.

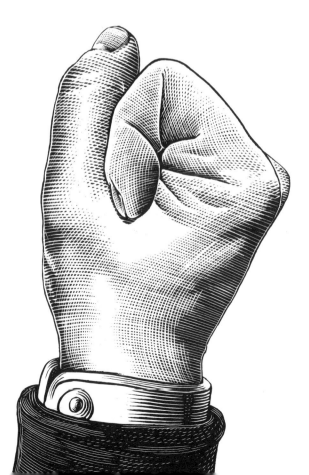

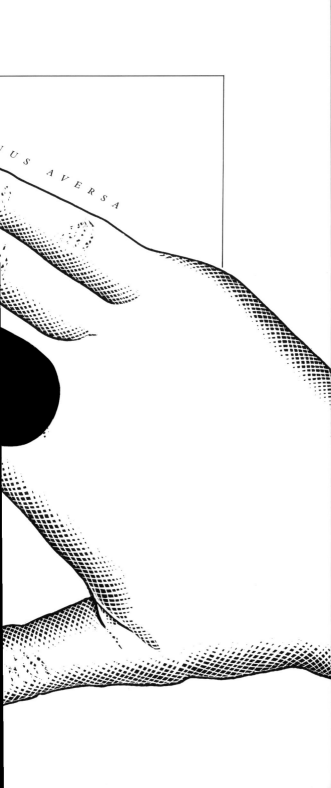

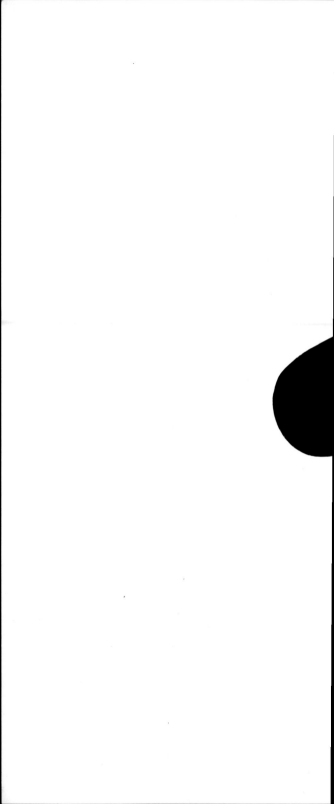

o being by the firm pinching up of loose
gers so used in this exposure. Further
ight parting movement of the said fingers,
ose skin situated on the back of the hand;
d to the hole all the while.

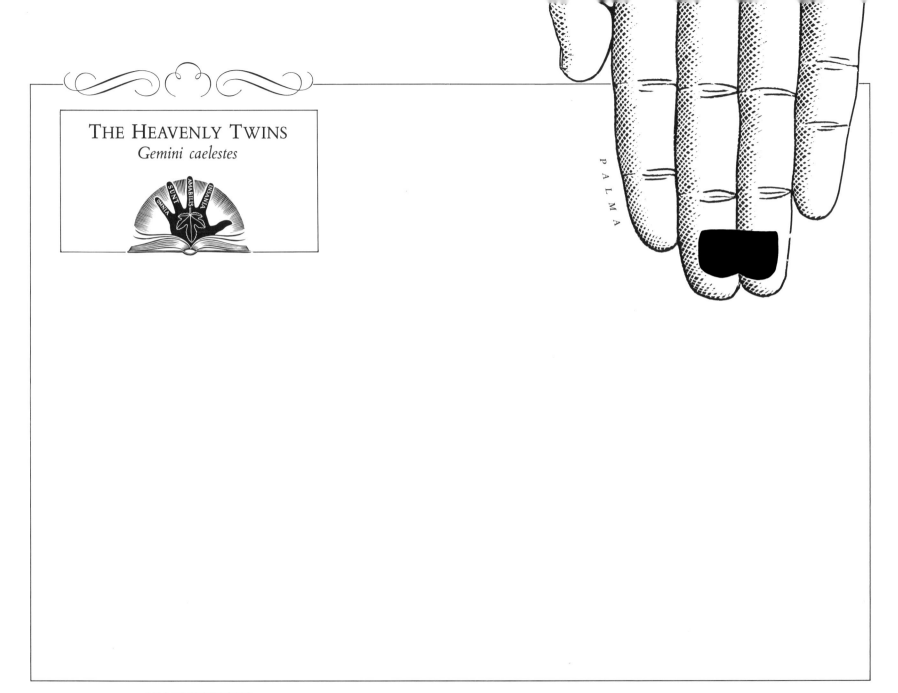

THE HEAVENLY TWINS
Gemini caelestes

PALMA

INSTRUCTIONS
Lift two pages and position the hand
underneath the hole in the manner shown in the diagram.
Turn the top page to expose.

A light application of saliva, occasioned by moistening the finger tips with the lips, will produce a wet appearance and so convey a quite admirble quality to the exposure.

DOBBIN'S DREAM
Tremor exquisitus

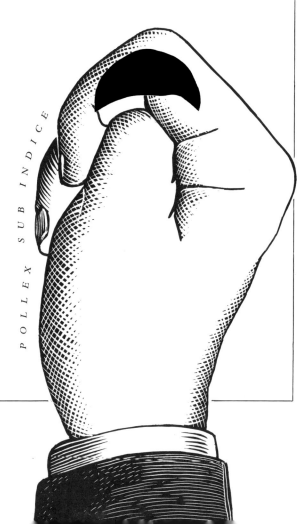

POLLEX SUB INDICE

INSTRUCTIONS
Lift two pages and position the hand
underneath the hole in the manner shown in the diagram.
Turn the top page to expose.

This exposure may be considerably invigorated by forward and backward movement of the thumb knuckle under the index finger. Such movement nicely replicates the riding motion in a manner most gratifying to the eye.

PLOUGHMAN'S FURROW
Fundamentum maximum

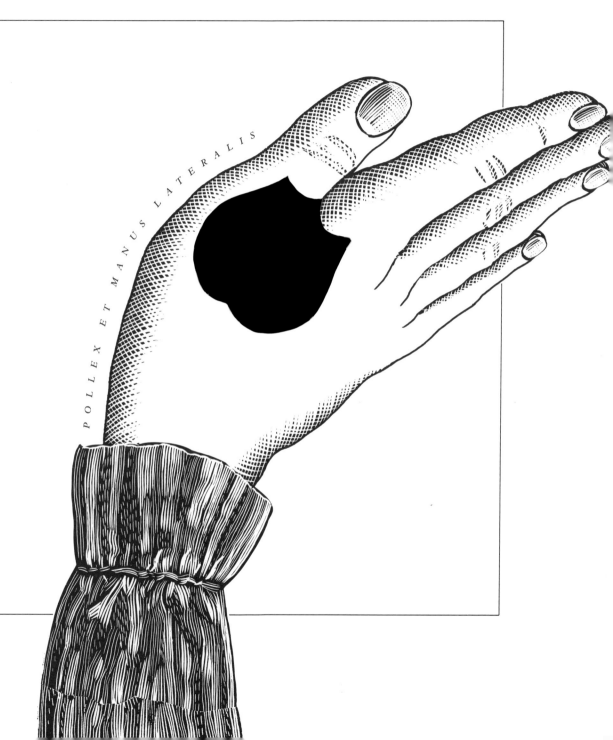

POLLEX ET MANUS LATERALIS

INSTRUCTIONS
Lift two pages and position the hand
underneath the hole in the manner shown in the diagram.
Turn the top page to expose.

*W*ith thumb and index finger squeezed tightly together, circular movement of the index finger will reward the diligent manipulator with most pleasing undulations of the protruberance. Allowing the flesh to protrude as far as is possible through the page will afford an area of exquisite sensation to the touch of the other hand.

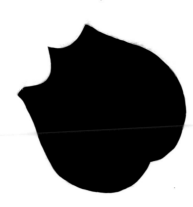

ROSEY PIE
Rosa erotica

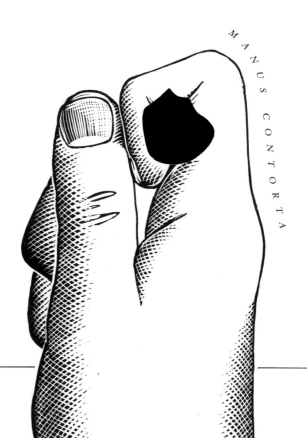

MANUS CONTORTA

INSTRUCTIONS
Lift two pages and position the hand
underneath the hole in the manner shown in the diagram.
Turn the top page to expose.

Vigorous lateral rubbing of this aspect with the open palm has been found to promote a most pleasingly youthful sheen. When the skin is of a moistness sufficient to resist such as sheen, however, a little talc applied sparingly to the index finger just prior to rubbing will greatly assist.

HAPPY VALLEY
Virgula denudata

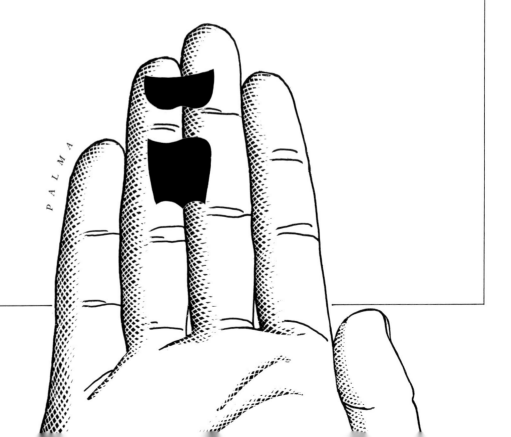

PALMA

INSTRUCTIONS
Lift two pages and position the hand
underneath the hole in the manner shown in the diagram.
Turn the top page to expose.

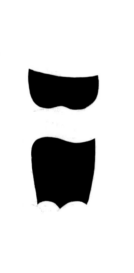

A strong light so positioned behind the palm as to infuse the cleft with a crimson glow (of a nature most appropriate to youth) is a thoroughly enjoyable elaboration of effect to be much admired.

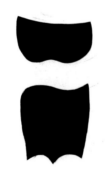

PINKY PUFF
Spongia voluptaria

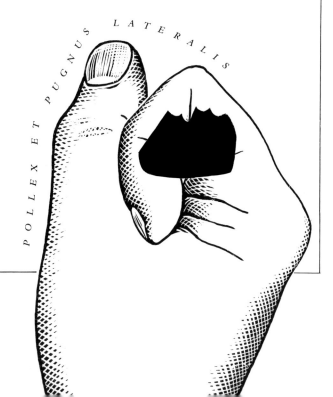

POLLEX ET PUGNUS LATERALIS

INSTRUCTIONS

Lift two pages and position the hand
underneath the hole in the manner shown in the diagram.
Turn the top page to expose.

Gentle squeezing of the index finger will infuse the area with a natural warm flush most pleasing to the eye. Again, the application of a little eau-de-Cologne will produce an agreeable glistening effect, rightly suggestive of skin bathed in sea water, while the perfume's fragrance lingering on the page will add enjoyment to future exposures.

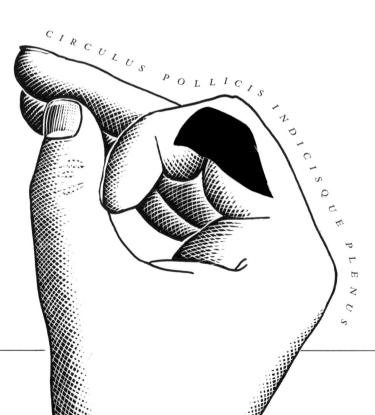

CIRCULUS POLLICIS INDICISQUE PLENUS

INSTRUCTIONS

Lift two pages and position the hand
underneath the hole in the manner shown in the diagram.
Turn the top page to expose.

The more creased nature of the skin to be found toward the base of the index finger is of a kind suggesting a flesh type of greater maturity. Those desirous of procuring this effect may move the finger forward a little, appropriate to the skin texture so required. The haired forearm also affords an agreeable alternative.

BOT PUDDING
Botellus pudicus

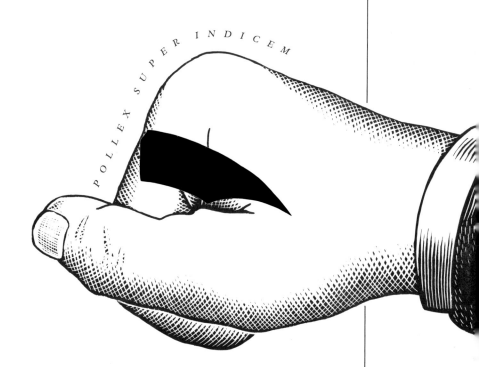

POLLEX SUPER INDICEM

INSTRUCTIONS
Lift two pages and position the hand
underneath the hole in the manner shown in the diagram.
Turn the top page to expose.

An interesting elaboration of this exposure is to be achieved by the alternate squeezing of thumb and index finger in such a manner as will result in muscular twitchings and pulsations of a most intriguing nature. In this respect some practice is requisite.

TONGUE AND CHEEKS
Membrum posterior

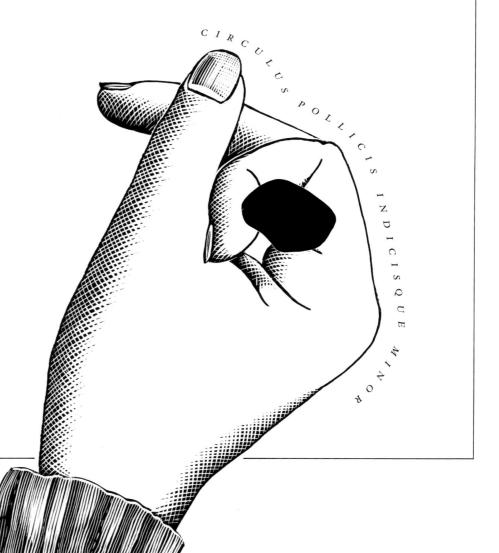

CIRCULUS POLLICIS INDICISQUE MINOR

INSTRUCTIONS
Lift two pages and position the hand
underneath the hole in the manner shown in the diagram.
Turn the top page to expose.

By subtle enlargement of the gap between the top joint of the index finger and its base, the little finger of the same hand may be allowed to wiggle about in the said gap, enabling a most real effect of considerable interest to be obtained.

GATES OF PARADISE
Portae paradisi

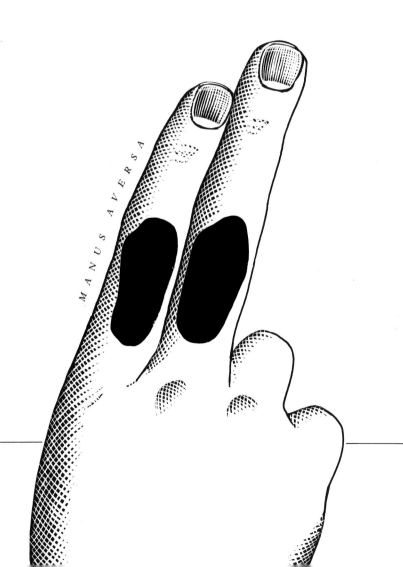

MANUS AVERSA

INSTRUCTIONS

Lift two pages and position the hand
underneath the hole in the manner shown in the diagram.
Turn the top page to expose.

A more youthful appearance may be engendered by the greater amount to which the knuckles are bent. Further it is desirable that the knuckles be encouraged to protrude as far as is possible, for, being placed thus more in evidence, they will evoke a most pleasurable realism.

FARMER'S FOLD
Fundamentum rotundum

POLLEX ET MANUS LATERALIS

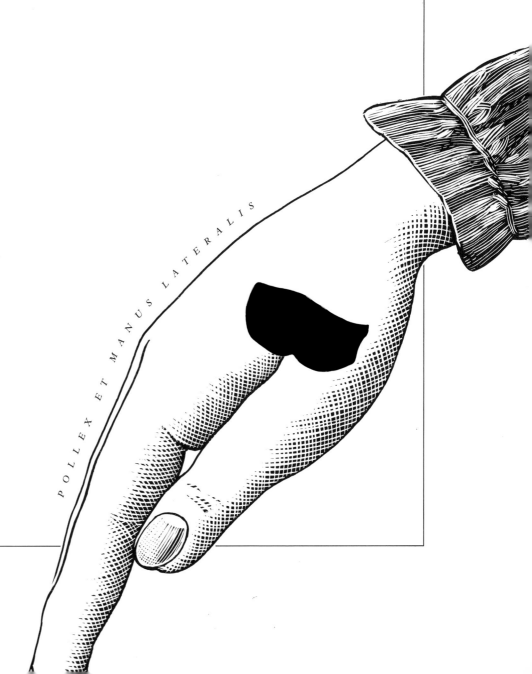

INSTRUCTIONS

Lift two pages and position the hand
underneath the hole in the manner shown in the diagram.
Turn the top page to expose.

A slow and circular parting movement of the thumb, with its concurrent muscular pulsations, greatly enhances this aspect. Further, the procurement of an oblique light source will nicely assist in the clear definition of any commodiously placed hairs.

 **Jeremy Bennett's** superb draughtsmanship and meticulous technique have already established this young artist as a leading New Zealand illustrator. His attention to detail, and the painstaking research he undertakes while completing the many preliminary sketches needed for each illustration, give his work an authenticity and a richness that will make this a book to be treasured.

 **Burton Silver** is a popular New Zealand cartoonist and problem-solver, well-known for his innovative creations and lateral ideas. This unique book is typical of his work, which has included the development of original concepts in such diverse areas as television, clothing, publishing, training schemes, road safety and social marketing.